Original title:
Tea Kettles and Twinkling Lights

Copyright © 2024 Creative Arts Management OÜ
All rights reserved.

Author: Elliot Harrison
ISBN HARDBACK: 978-9916-94-416-5
ISBN PAPERBACK: 978-9916-94-417-2

Comforting Mists Under Starlit Dreams

The night wraps round like a soft embrace,
Gentle mists waltz in a twilight dance.
Stars above twinkle with grace,
Filling the hearts with a hopeful glance.

Whispers of calm in the cool night air,
Guiding souls to a tranquil rest.
In dreams, we wander without a care,
Finding solace in the night's gentle chest.

Illuminated Moments of Calm

In the fading glow of the evening light,
Soft shadows stretch, dancing low.
Moments of peace, pure and bright,
Invite our hearts to gently flow.

Breath of the night, a soothing balm,
Crickets sing in a harmonious hymn.
Every heartbeat offers a calm,
In these moments, the world seems dim.

Whispers of Boiling Dreams

A kettle whistles in the quiet space,
Thoughts simmering, waiting to be stirred.
Dreams bubble up in a warm embrace,
Actions whispered, softly heard.

In the rush of life, the steam does rise,
Carrying hopes in delicate trails.
Through the chaos, we seek the prize,
In boiling dreams, our spirit sails.

Glimmers in the Steam

In the steam, glimmers of light,
Dancing shadows in a twisted play.
Each flicker whispers of delight,
Memories rising, drifting away.

Capturing time in a fleeting glow,
Fleeting moments, elusive and sweet.
In the vapor, our feelings flow,
Finding solace in the warmth of heat.

The Glow Within the Pot

In shadows cast by evening's light,
A kettle hums, warmth ignites.
With fragrant herbs and gentle steam,
A cozy cup fulfills the dream.

The amber hue of liquid gold,
Stories shared, both shy and bold.
With every sip, comfort flows,
The heart finds rest, the spirit grows.

Dreaming of Warm Wishes

In quiet nights, when stars align,
We wish for warmth, a love divine.
Through whispered prayers and softest dreams,
Hope dances bright in moonlit beams.

With every thought, we send our care,
Through distant lands, on evening air.
Wrapped in kindness, wrapped in light,
We find our way, through darkest night.

Laughter over Glimmering Mugs

Around the table, joy does bloom,
With mugs in hand, dispelling gloom.
Laughter rings, like bells on high,
As stories sing and spirits fly.

The warmth of drink, the glow of cheer,
Uniting hearts, bringing us near.
In every sip, a memory made,
In this lovely bond, we won't trade.

Froth and Flicker Under the Moon

Beneath the stars, the moonlight glows,
Frothy dreams in soft repose.
Candles flicker, shadows dance,
In quiet moments, hearts entranced.

With every breath, the night unfolds,
A tapestry of whispers told.
In stillness deep, we find our sighs,
Froth and flicker, beneath the skies.

Steamy Stories from Warm Pottery

In the hearth where clay meets fire,
Whispers of warmth, a soft desire.
Mugs in hand, we cradle dreams,
Stories brewed in smoky seams.

Laughter dances on the steam,
Pottery holds each glimmering theme.
Fingers trace the edges worn,
In this moment, we are reborn.

Textures tell as spirits flow,
In the night, we watch the glow.
Each sip a tale, a cherished lore,
The pottery speaks, forevermore.

Together we weave, hand in hand,
In the steam, our hearts make stand.
The stories linger, soft and sweet,
In the whispers of the warm retreat.

The Fable of Mug and Candle

Mug of clay, warm and round,
Beside a candle, softly found.
Flame flickers, shadows play,
Together they light up the gray.

In quiet nights, they share their glow,
Whispers shared, secrets flow.
Candle stands with light so bold,
While the mug holds warmth, like gold.

Once they dreamed of distant lands,
Where coffee brews and comfort stands.
In the stillness, stories blend,
Mug and candle, the perfect friend.

Fables spun in liquid sigh,
Underneath the moonlit sky.
Each night together, they ignite,
A timeless tale of soft delight.

Echoes of Steam Among the Glimmers

Amid the glimmers, steam arises,
Whispers of life, sweet surprises.
Beneath the arches, echoes call,
In the glow, we find our all.

Each breath a note, each sip a song,
Echoes linger, where we belong.
Tea leaves dance in a porcelain sea,
In the moment, we are free.

The kettle sings, a melodious hum,
Filling the room with warmth to come.
Glimmers spark in every eye,
Steam wraps softly, a tender sigh.

In this place, we weave our dreams,
Echoes linger in gentle streams.
Together, hearts beat with grace,
In the steam, we find our place.

The Echoing Melody of Warmth

In the stillness of the night,
Soft whispers start to rise.
A longing in the shadows,
A tune that never dies.

Each note a tender feather,
That falls without a sound.
It dances on the breezes,
Where love and peace abound.

The warmth becomes a blanket,
That wraps around the heart.
Echoes through the silence,
A melody, a start.

With every gentle heartbeat,
The music swells inside.
A symphony of dreaming,
Where hope and joy reside.

Luminous Moments in a Quiet Cup

In a vessel full of comfort,
Beneath the morning light,
A hint of warmth and sweetness,
Moments pure and bright.

The steam curls in the air,
A dance of dreams and thoughts.
Sipping slow, embracing
The magic that it brought.

Each sip a gentle whisper,
A story yet untold.
Luminous and alive,
A treasure to behold.

In a quiet cup, we gather,
The peace our souls design.
In every savory flavor,
We find a love divine.

Sipping Serenity Under Shimmering Skies

Beneath the vast expanse,
Where stars begin to glow,
We find a sense of solace,
In moments soft and slow.

With every gentle sip,
The world fades far away.
The night ignites with charm,
In a soothing ballet.

Serenity surrounds us,
As stars twinkle and gleam.
The sky a velvet blanket,
Sheltering our dream.

Each drop a flowing river,
Where peace and hope entwine.
Sipping under starlight,
A treasure so divine.

The Gentle Caress of Fire and Glow

Where embers softly whisper,
And shadows start to dance,
The warmth of fire's embrace,
Entraps us in a trance.

Flickering flames ignite,
A glow that sets us free.
Each spark a fleeting moment,
A glimpse of destiny.

The gentle caress of heat,
As night begins to fall.
Wrapped in warmth and wonder,
We hear the fire's call.

The essence of its magic,
A comfort we adore.
With firelight as our beacon,
We long for nothing more.

A Serene Brew Beneath the Stars

In the stillness, night unfolds,
Whispers of dreams, gently told.
Stars shine bright, a guiding light,
Comfort found in this quiet night.

A cup of warmth in tender hands,
Silhouettes cast on soft sands.
Moonlight dances in swirling brew,
Each sip a promise, old yet new.

The world pauses, time feels slow,
In this moment, love can grow.
Beneath the cosmos, hearts align,
Brewed serenity, simply divine.

Sparkling Moments in a Warm Embrace

In laughter shared, a sparkle gleams,
Moments weaving through our dreams.
Arms entwined, hearts beat as one,
In your warmth, my fears are done.

Soft whispers float on evening air,
Every glance, a silent prayer.
Together we chase the twilight hues,
Every second, love renews.

The world outside fades away,
Together is where we choose to stay.
In your glow, all worries cease,
Sparkling moments, my heart's peace.

The Heartbeat of Warmth and Light

In the glow of fading dusk,
Familiar warmth, simple trust.
Hearts entwined, a steady beat,
In our home, life feels complete.

Golden rays through windowpanes,
Whispers of love, soft refrains.
Each corner holds a memory sweet,
In this space, our souls repeat.

Breath of laughter fills the air,
Every glance, a tender stare.
Together we shine, hope ignites,
The heartbeat of warmth and light.

Midnight Rituals with Eloquent Steam

Under stars, the kettle sings,
Magic dances, the night brings.
Eloquent steam, rising slow,
Whispers of warmth in a steady flow.

Each pour, a moment divine,
Memories brewed, yours and mine.
In this ritual, peace unfurls,
Night embraces, as time twirls.

With every sip, our spirits meet,
In the stillness, hearts retreat.
Midnight's call, we softly share,
In each cup, our dreams declare.

Fragrant Haze of Gentle Chatter

In the morning sun's embrace,
We gather near, smiles on our face.
Whispers dance in soft delight,
Carried on the breeze so light.

Stories weave, a tapestry so bright,
Laughter twinkles like stars at night.
Time drifts gently on soft wings,
As heart to heart, the joy it brings.

Underneath the shady trees,
With each word, the world agrees.
Fragrant haze of coffee steam,
In these moments, we all dream.

As daylight fades, and shadows roam,
In every laugh, we find our home.
These gentle chats, a bond so rare,
A fragrant haze beyond compare.

A Cascade of Shimmering Thoughts

In quiet pools of moonlit grace,
Ideas ripple, a timeless chase.
Shimmering visions take to flight,
Whispers merge in the still of night.

Each thought a drop that falls so free,
Creating waves of possibility.
In the silence, clarity unfolds,
A cascade of dreams, bold and untold.

Echoes of wonder fill the air,
Painting pictures beyond compare.
Mind's canvas bright, with colors true,
A cascade of thoughts, old and new.

Let the ideas freely flow,
In this moment, let them grow.
In the dance of shadows, we embrace,
A shimmering world, a sacred space.

Celestial Comfort in Each Sip

With every cup, a story brews,
Hints of cocoa, or berry hues.
Warmth wraps round like a cherished friend,
Celestial comfort that won't end.

Steam rising like whispers at dawn,
In stillness, the world's worries are gone.
Each sip a journey, rich and deep,
Waking dreams from quiet sleep.

Lost in flavors that softly blend,
In every taste, the heart will mend.
Moments linger, sweet and rare,
In each embrace, love fills the air.

As dusk descends, and day takes flight,
In the glow of stars, we find our light.
Celestial comfort, deep and vast,
In every sip, memories cast.

Alight in the Midnight Brew

When the world sleeps, and silence reigns,
A kettle sings, easing the strains.
Darkness shimmers with liquid gold,
Alight in warmth, stories unfold.

Flecked with spice, and sweetness too,
Each cup brings promise, fresh as dew.
Tales of old and hopes anew,
In the midnight brew, dreams come true.

Shadows dance, as laughter flows,
With every sip, the spirit grows.
Together, we conquer fears once brew,
In the still of night, our hearts imbue.

So raise a cup, let worries cease,
In the magic of this warm release.
Alight in the night, we'll find our crew,
In every measure of the midnight brew.

Celestial Warmth in a Cup

A sip of sun in porcelain,
Golden rays in liquid form.
Each drop brings the sky closer,
A cozy hug, blissful and warm.

Steam rises like whispered dreams,
Dancing softly in the air.
Comfort found in every taste,
A moment's peace, beyond compare.

Ceramic glow beneath the stars,
Guiding hearts to the divine.
In every cup, a galaxy,
A universe, yours and mine.

With every drink, bliss unfolds,
Celestial warmth, pure and bright.
In these moments, time stands still,
Embracing love in the night.

Light Sparks in the Night

Stars twinkle in velvet deep,
Each a story, softly told.
They dance in the cosmic weave,
Whispers of dreams, bright and bold.

Moonbeams play on silver lakes,
Casting shadows, bold and fair.
In the hush of the cool night,
Magic lingers in the air.

A flicker here, a shimmer there,
Life ignites with every spark.
Hearts ignite in quiet tones,
Lighting pathways through the dark.

Beneath the vast, endless sky,
Hope like starlight fills the space.
Moments shine, then fade away,
But in memories, they trace.

The Melodies of Hot Metal

In the forge, the hammer sings,
Clashing with the fire's breath.
Sparks fly like a symphony,
Creating beauty from the depth.

Rhythms pulse in molten gold,
Shapes emerge from blazing heat.
Each strike tells of strength and skill,
Crafting destiny, bittersweet.

Whispers weave through iron veins,
Songs of labor, grit, and grace.
A dance of hands, a labor's birth,
In this space, we find our place.

As metal cools, the echoes fade,
But melodies, they linger near.
In the heart of every piece,
The music swells, strong and clear.

Radiance Above the Hearth

In the glow of the evening fire,
Embers dance with passionate grace.
A warm embrace of fleeting light,
Filling hearts, a sacred space.

Above the hearth, shadows play,
Stories wrapped in crackling sound.
In flickering warmth, we gather close,
In this haven, love is found.

Sweet aromas fill the air,
From cooking meals, hearty and bold.
Each flavor a tale, each bite a hug,
Nourishing the stories told.

As the night wraps us in dreams,
Radiance hums, a vibrant thread.
In togetherness, we find our home,
In love's glow, forever fed.

Mellow Evenings and Enchanted Brews

As daylight fades to twilight's glow,
A gentle breeze begins to blow.
The stars awaken, soft and bright,
Mellow evenings bring pure delight.

Teacups clink in cozy nooks,
Within the glow of cherished books.
Whispers dance in the fading light,
As magic weaves through the night.

Warm aromas fill the air,
With laughter shared, beyond compare.
Soothing sips of herbal tea,
Mellow evenings set us free.

With every brew, our spirits lift,
In moments shared, the greatest gift.
Enchanted nights, we gently toast,
To friendships held, we cherish most.

Elysium in Every Steam Cloud

In the morning's gentle light,
Steam arises, pure delight.
Each cup spills dreams, a sacred flow,
Elysium found in every dro.

A dance of flavors intertwine,
In every sip, a taste divine.
A fragrant journey, warm and bold,
Stories whispered, dreams retold.

With every swan of creamy foam,
Hearts find peace, a cozy home.
Together here, the world feels right,
In steam clouds, find sheer delight.

As moments pass, we cherish this,
The joy of brews, a simple bliss.
Elysium flows in cups we share,
In every heartbeat, love and care.

Radiance in the Heart of a Brew

In the kettle, colors bloom,
A radiant dance dispels the gloom.
With glowing warmth in every cup,
Life's sweet moments, we drink up.

Golden hues that softly shine,
In every swirl, our lives align.
Stories linger, softly spun,
In each warm brew, we become one.

With laughter shared and peace anew,
There's magic found in every brew.
A gentle heart, a warming light,
Radiance flows through day and night.

Together we create a spark,
In the quiet, we leave our mark.
With each sip, a love that's true,
Radiance lives in the heart of a brew.

Glowing Secrets Unveiled

As evening settles, shadows fall,
In glowing brews, the night calls.
Secrets whispered, soft and low,
In every cup, a tale will flow.

Flavors mingle, rich and rare,
In every sip, love fills the air.
Crafted moments, shared so sweet,
Secrets glow where friends all meet.

A dance of light in porcelain white,
Under stars, our dreams take flight.
Every flavor, a story spun,
Glowing secrets shared by everyone.

As laughter echoes in the dark,
We sip and savor, leave a mark.
With glowing hearts, we embrace the night,
In shared brews, we find our light.

A Symphony of Glow

In twilight's gentle touch, we find,
The whispers of the stars aligned.
Each shimmer tells a tale of old,
A symphony of dreams unfolds.

With every flicker, hearts ignite,
A dance of shadows in the night.
The moon, a witness to our souls,
Plays chords of light, makes us whole.

Together, we embrace the skies,
With laughter echoing, love replies.
The colors blend, a vibrant show,
In this, our symphony of glow.

Liquid Comfort Under Luminescence

Beneath the glow of evening's light,
We find our peace, our hearts take flight.
The liquid warmth in gentle streams,
Invites us to explore our dreams.

With each soft ripple, calm descends,
Water's embrace, where sorrow mends.
In quiet pools, reflections bloom,
A world of solace begins to loom.

Under stars that softly gleam,
We sip from life, a soothing dream.
In liquid comfort, we unite,
Awash in love, beneath the night.

Echoes of the Evening Boil

The kettle sings, a call to gather,
In rising steam, we find our chatter.
Whispers dance along the brew,
Echoes warm, like morning dew.

In every cup, a heart we share,
The evening glow, a fragrant air.
We stir the night with laughter light,
As stories blend within our sight.

Bubbling tales in harmony,
Each sip brings forth sweet memory.
In evening's hold, we intertwine,
Echoes linger, love's design.

Radiant Reflections

In pools of silver, dreams collide,
Reflections cast in tranquil tide.
Each ripple tells a story bright,
A canvas painted with pure light.

As dawn ascends to greet the day,
Radiant hues begin to play.
In every glance, the world transforms,
A symphony of beauty warms.

We chase the light, our hearts align,
In every moment, love will shine.
With radiant reflections clear,
We find our joy, our path is here.

Sparks of Warmth in the Dark

In the shadows soft and deep,
Flickers dance where secrets keep.
Glows of amber, whispers low,
Hearts entwined in gentle flow.

Every spark ignites the night,
Filling souls with pure delight.
In the silence, love will bloom,
Lighting paths through endless gloom.

Cozy Embrace of Bright Nights

Stars are stitched in velvet skies,
Holding dreams in tender ties.
Wrapped in warmth, we sit and sigh,
Beneath the moon's soft lullaby.

Cups of cocoa, laughter shared,
Every moment, love declared.
In this haven, time stands still,
All that matters is this thrill.

Inside the Hearth's Whisper

Crackling fire, a glowing face,
Softened light, a warm embrace.
Stories told of years gone by,
Echoed gently, low and high.

Ashes dance, revealing grace,
Memory's warmth in this space.
Through the flickers, voices blend,
In the hearth, time has no end.

Tales from Steam-kissed Dreams

Mugs are steaming, filled with cheer,
Whispers swirl, drawing us near.
In the twilight, fables weave,
Every tale, a heart to grieve.

Time suspended, magic flows,
In the mist, our wonder grows.
With each sip, a world unfolds,
Crafting dreams in cozy molds.

Stars Whispering in Cerulean

In the hush of night, they gleam,
Each one a distant, whispered dream.
They dance in skies, vast and deep,
Secrets of the cosmos they keep.

A canvas brushed with silver sighs,
Softly twinkling in endless skies.
They guide the way, a lantern bright,
Stars whisper tales in lunar light.

Through velvet shadows, they invite,
A serenade of shimmering light.
With every flicker, hearts align,
In Celestial realms, love divine.

Eternal watchers, pure and free,
In their glow, we find our glee.
Beneath their gaze, the world will glow,
In cerulean dreams, we ebb and flow.

The Embrace of Warmth and Glow

In early morn, the sun will rise,
With golden beams that fill the skies.
A gentle touch on waking life,
A promise bright, free of strife.

The warmth of day, a soft caress,
In every heart, a sweet success.
The glow of laughter fills the air,
A world embraced, beyond compare.

As evening falls, hues weave and blend,
In twilight's arms, the day will end.
Hearts wrapped in comfort, peace will flow,
In every sinew, warmth we know.

Together, in the fading light,
We gather hope against the night.
In every hug, the love we sow,
The beauty found in warmth and glow.

Harmonies at the Edge of Twilight

As day concedes, the night draws near,
Soft melodies for hearts to hear.
The sun dips low, a golden hue,
Twilight sings its song so true.

Shadows stretch across the land,
A symphony at twilight's hand.
Crisp notes linger on the breeze,
Time slows down with graceful ease.

Crickets chirp in rhythmic tune,
While fireflies dance beneath the moon.
Nature hums a lullaby,
In twilight's grasp, we softly sigh.

Under stars, the world stands still,
Harmony in every thrill.
A sacred moment, calm and bright,
In twilight's embrace, pure delight.

Shining Moments in Rustic Existence

In fields where wildflowers grow,
Simple joys begin to flow.
The rustic charm of life unfolds,
In every story, warmth retold.

A wooden porch, the sun sets low,
With laughter shared, sweet memories grow.
The crackle of the evening fire,
In every spark, our hearts aspire.

With every dawn, fresh tales arise,
Life's gentle rhythm never lies.
In moments spent beneath the trees,
We find our peace, our hearts at ease.

Through winding paths and whispering streams,
Rustic life fulfills our dreams.
In nature's arms, we find our song,
In shining moments, we belong.

Solitude Bathed in Soft Gleam

In the quiet night, I roam,
Soft moonlight guides me home.
Shadows dance upon the ground,
In solitude, peace is found.

Gentle whispers fill the air,
Thoughts wander without a care.
Each star a distant, twinkling gem,
In this embrace, I find my stem.

Nature sings her lullaby,
While the world holds its sigh.
Bathed in gleam, I'm not alone,
In this stillness, love has grown.

As dawn breaks, the light will share,
The secrets of the night laid bare.
But for now, I cherish deep,
This solitude I always keep.

Histories in a Hot Embrace

In the furnace of the past,
Lovers' whispers hold me fast.
Lives entwined in golden threads,
Embers glow where passion treads.

Time holds memories like a flame,
Each touch whispers a sweet name.
In the heat, our stories weave,
Histories born with hearts that believe.

Fingers trace the scars we wear,
Tales of joy, deep sorrow's share.
In this warmth, I feel alive,
In our embrace, we always thrive.

A tapestry of days gone by,
Underneath the endless sky.
Together we craft our dreams,
In the night, our love redeems.

Sipping Stories Beneath Stars

Beneath the stars, our secrets flow,
In gentle laughter, soft and slow.
Sipping dreams from porcelain cups,
In this moment, time erupts.

Each story told, a thread unwinds,
In the galaxy, our fate aligns.
With every sip, a world we build,
In moonlit tales, our hearts are filled.

Whispers float on the evening breeze,
In shared glances, we find our ease.
Every star a memory bright,
Guiding us through the velvety night.

As dawn approaches, we'll hold tight,
To these tales that make us light.
In quiet moments, we will find,
A universe that's intertwined.

Glows of Warmth and Whispered Ambiance

In the glow of candlelight,
Whispers dance, hearts take flight.
Wrapped in warmth, the night feels deep,
Promises made are ours to keep.

Flickering flames, shadows play,
Every glance, a word to say.
In the silence, feelings grow,
In the ambiance, soft and slow.

Laughter glimmers, bright and free,
A symphony, just you and me.
Comfort found in softer tones,
In this haven, love has grown.

As the night begins to wane,
In our hearts, it will remain.
Guided by the glow so pure,
In whispered warmth, we feel secure.

Silk and Silver in Liquid Form

Silken threads of moonlight flash,
Rippling on the quiet stream,
Silver whispers weave a splash,
In the gentle night's soft dream.

A dance of shadows, soft and light,
Caressing banks with tender grace,
Liquid gems in silver plight,
Flowing through the night's embrace.

Each droplet holds a story dear,
Of secret wishes, deep desire,
Echoed laughter, hushed yet clear,
In the depths, hearts never tire.

As stars above begin to glow,
The waters shimmer, kiss the shore,
In silk and silver's quiet flow,
Eternity is offered more.

Odes to Charmed Respite

In the sanctuary of the trees,
A hush, a calm, where dreams take flight,
Whispers carried on the breeze,
Charmed respite in soft twilight.

Golden rays in warm embrace,
Cradle thoughts like rolling dew,
Nature's arms, a loving space,
Where solitude feels fresh and new.

Clouds drift slowly overhead,
Promises painted in the sky,
In these moments, worries shed,
Time unfolds, and worries die.

To linger here, a cherished boon,
In brows of dusk, sweet peace entwined,
The heart alights to silent tunes,
In every whisper, life defined.

Glinting Spheres of Late-Night Solace

Beneath the velvet shroud of night,
Stars emerge like scattered dreams,
Glinting spheres, a wondrous sight,
Casting down their silver beams.

The moon, a guardian up above,
Watches over all below,
With every ray, a tale of love,
In serene beauty, hearts must glow.

Each twinkle holds a moment lost,
In the quiet, secrets keep,
In solitude, though at a cost,
The cosmos sings the night to sleep.

Embrace this solace, sweet and rare,
Find your peace within the stars,
In the darkness, light is fair,
Late-night whispers heal old scars.

Reflections of Light in Hot Embrace

Sunset paints the world in fire,
Golden hues that melt the day,
Waves of warmth enkindled desire,
As shadows dance and softly sway.

Flames flicker with a wild grace,
In their glow, the night unfolds,
A tapestry of time and space,
With stories that the darkness holds.

Hearts are warmed by the blazing light,
In this haven, troubles cease,
Embraced by warmth that feels so right,
In every glance, a moment's peace.

The fire crackles, soft and low,
Each spark a memory, a trace,
In the night, our spirits grow,
In reflections of light's warm embrace.

Bright Horizons in Cups of Joy

In morning light, they gleam so bright,
Each cup a promise, a new delight.
With every sip, a dream takes flight,
Joy's embrace in colors bright.

Moments shared, laughter flows,
Feelings warm as sunlight glows.
The world awakens, hope bestows,
In cups of joy, love surely grows.

Steam rises, whispers in the air,
Fragile dreams, tender care.
Savoring each, a heartfelt dare,
In every drop, memories we share.

A toast to life, to friends, to cheer,
In vibrant cups, we hold so dear.
With every sip, we draw more near,
Bright horizons, wholly clear.

Fluid Artistry of Heat and Reflection

Colors swirl, a canvas bold,
With gentle heat, the stories unfold.
A dance of hues, both warm and cold,
Artistry of fluid, vividly told.

Reflections bounce, the light does play,
Every curve, a story's sway.
In molten dreams, we find the way,
To capture moments, night and day.

Creative tides, a passionate flow,
In every piece, emotions glow.
Chasing shadows and afterglow,
The artistry thrives, and we bestow.

In harmony, we blend and merge,
With fervent hearts, we feel the surge.
Through heat and light, our spirits urge,
To shape the world, our dreams emerge.

The Dance of Light and Liquid

Light cascades on waves of blue,
In liquid grace, the world renews.
A gentle dance, a sparkling view,
Nature's rhythm, pure and true.

Reflections twist, the surface sways,
In every ripple, magic plays.
Sunset hues in golden rays,
A symphony through night and days.

Liquid whispers, a soft refrain,
In echoes sweet, the heart's domain.
With every splash, we break the chain,
In life's embrace, love's sweet gain.

We find our rhythm, flow like streams,
In every droplet, silent dreams.
Together moving, life's bright beams,
In this dance, we find our themes.

A Serenade in Every Sip

A warm embrace in every cup,
Each sip a song, we lift it up.
Notes of spice, and sweetness sup,
In every drop, we find our luck.

With swirls of flavor, hearts entwine,
Stories whispered, aged like wine.
In silence shared, two souls align,
A serenade in liquid fine.

Moments linger, like a tune,
Beneath the light of a silver moon.
A fleeting glance, love's sweet monsoon,
In every sip, our hearts attune.

Raise your glass, let's toast tonight,
In every drop, the world feels right.
Together, we'll chase away the fright,
With every sip, our dreams ignite.

Nighttime Chimes in Porcelain

Under moonlit skies they sing,
Softly through the night they ring,
Whispers of the stars' embrace,
Time suspended in this space.

Porcelain dreams that gently sway,
Echoes of the past betray,
Tales of love and fleeting time,
In the air, a subtle rhyme.

Gentle hands that hold the light,
In the hush of quiet night,
Chimes that dance in breezy air,
Carrying secrets everywhere.

While the world is fast asleep,
Melodies in shadows creep,
Nighttime's lullaby is cast,
Porcelain songs that hold us fast.

Twilight's Sipping Song

The sky blushes with twilight's hue,
Moments linger, soft and true,
Sipping on the day's last light,
Whispers weave through gentle night.

Colors blend in dusk's sweet kiss,
Every note a fleeting bliss,
Nature breathes in tender tones,
Harmony in whispered moans.

A cup of stars, the moon's delight,
Sipping dreams in purest flight,
While the world begins to fade,
Twilight's song won't ever trade.

Laughter blends with twilight's breath,
Celebrating life and death,
In this moment, rich and long,
Lost in twilight's sipping song.

Laughter in the Faintest Flicker

A candle glows with warmth inside,
Hope and dreams begin to bide,
Laughter dances with the flame,
In the whisper of its name.

Flickers paint the walls with light,
Glimmers soft as stars at night,
Echoes of a playful cheer,
Softest giggles draw us near.

In shadows, secrets find their ground,
Faintest flickers, joy unbound,
Light that flickers, laughs that soar,
In this moment, we want more.

Time may fade, but here we stay,
Laughter holds the night at bay,
In the warmth of tender glow,
Faintest flickers, love will grow.

The Glow of Comfort Brews

A teapot sings in cozy hue,
Steam rising, warmth slips through,
Sipping soft, the world slows down,
In this glow, we both have found.

Cup in hand, the evening calls,
Embers dance as daylight falls,
Stories shared beneath the light,
Filling hearts with pure delight.

Comfort flows in every sip,
Moments linger, time won't slip,
In this space, we know so well,
The glow of comfort casts its spell.

As shadows stretch across the room,
Love brews deeper, banishing gloom,
In the warmth, we draw so close,
In the glow of comfort, we toast.

Whispers in the Steel

Beneath the cold, the echoes hum,
A tale of strength where dreams succumb.
Silence weaves through rust and grime,
In shadows cast, we march through time.

The iron giants stand so tall,
Guarding secrets, great and small.
With every clang, they whisper low,
The heartbeats of the steel we know.

In twilight's glow, the forge ignites,
Turning dark to brilliant sights.
The dance of metal, fire's art,
Each spark a song that moves the heart.

Whispers linger, tales retold,
In every grain, a story bold.
The steel remembers, never fears,
A serenade through countless years.

Celestial Brews

Stars drip down like honeyed light,
In cosmic cups that brew the night.
Galaxies swirl in fragrant dreams,
Where stardust dances and moonlight gleams.

With every sip, a twilight glow,
The universe in rhythms flow.
Nebulas blend in fragrant steam,
A sip of wonder, a cosmic dream.

Time unravels in sips so rare,
As constellations twirl in air.
Brewing warmth from distant lands,
In every drop, the cosmos stands.

Celestial brews, our spirits rise,
In every taste, the vast, the wise.
We gather close, as shadows cast,
In sips of futures, present, past.

Glimmers of Warmth

In chilly air, the whispers trace,
The flicker of a soft embrace.
Fires crackle, shadows dance,
Inviting hearts to take a chance.

The golden glow like sunlit dreams,
A tapestry of light that beams.
Through frosted panes, the warmth streams in,
A shelter found, where love begins.

Ember's glow and gentle sighs,
In tender moments, laughter flies.
Glimmers spark in every eye,
As winter fades and spirits fly.

Together here, we weave our song,
In glimmers bright, where we belong.
With every heartbeat, warmth unfolds,
A quilt of stories, courage bold.

The Dance of Steam and Stars

In the quiet night, the steam ascends,
Blending softly, where silence bends.
Stars wink down, a twinkling gaze,
Pulsing rhythms, a sacred praise.

From kettle's spout, a fragrant sigh,
As steam curls up towards the sky.
Whirling patterns in a cosmic trance,
Connect the heavens in a dance.

With every swirl, the night ignites,
A symphony of gentle lights.
The universe joins in a twirling spree,
In steam and stars, we find the key.

Let us drink deep from this celestial brew,
In every moment, find what's true.
For in the dance of steam and stars,
We discover who we really are.

Candlelit Conversations

Whispers dance in gentle light,
Flickers tease the shadows tight.
Thoughts drift softly through the air,
Secrets shared, a tender care.

Eyes that shimmer like the flame,
Voices hushed, hearts call each name.
Moments pause as time suspends,
In this glow, the world transcends.

Echoes linger, warmth remains,
In the light, our joy proclaims.
Soft reflections on your face,
In this space, we find our place.

Beneath the stars, our dreams ignite,
Candlelit, we embrace the night.

Chasing Shadows with Steam

Morning mist hugs the quiet ground,
Whispers of the night, unbound.
Steam rises, cloaks the day,
Chasing shadows, lost at play.

Footsteps echo, soft and low,
In the haze, where secrets grow.
Memories wrapped in vapor tight,
Dreams unfold, then take to flight.

Time drips slowly, moments blend,
Steam and shadows, they transcend.
Fading figures, lost from view,
In this dance, I chase the true.

Light breaks through, a gentle ray,
Chasing shadows, night gives way.

A Symphony of Heat and Glow

Fires crackle, warmth we know,
In the hearth, a vibrant show.
Notes of comfort fill the air,
In harmony, we pause and stare.

Rhythms pulse like beating hearts,
Each flicker, where the magic starts.
Glowing embers paint the night,
In this symphony, pure delight.

Songs of warmth, the quiet kind,
In the glow, we seek, we find.
Threads of laughter weave their way,
In this glow, we wish to stay.

As the darkness starts to fall,
We find our peace, our warmth, our all.

Stars in a Porcelain Sky

Porcelain dreams in midnight's glow,
Stars like whispers, soft and slow.
Each a wish, a tale untold,
In this canvas, visions bold.

Twinkling lights, a serene sea,
Where the heart finds joy and free.
Cradled in the night's embrace,
Every star, a sacred place.

Gentle breezes, cool and clear,
Carry secrets, drawing near.
Lucid moments as they gleam,
In this sky, we dream our dream.

Porcelain stars, so brightly speak,
In their glow, we find the meek.

Aroma of Dusk and Dawn

The sky blushes deep, a twilight hue,
Whispers of night come softly anew.
Fragrant blooms breathe life in the air,
In the stillness, dreams begin to dare.

Stars awaken, twinkling bright,
Beneath the horizon, a dance of light.
The dawn will tease with colors bold,
As night retreats, its stories told.

Aromatic spices, the world held dear,
In laughter and warmth, we draw near.
With every moment, time unfolds,
In the aroma of dusk, life beholds.

A fleeting embrace, both tender and soft,
Between the chaos, we find our loft.
In the twilight's breath, we find a way,
To cherish the dusk, to greet the day.

The Soft Purr of Embered Whispers

In the heart of night, embers glow,
Soft purrs of warmth begin to flow.
Hidden tales by the firelight told,
Echoes of secrets, both new and old.

Gentle shadows flicker and dance,
As whispers entwine in a fragile trance.
The night holds its breath, a moment shy,
While stars weave dreams in the velvet sky.

Silhouettes of memories in the flame,
Each flicker a pulse, each spark a name.
In tender embrace, we sit side by side,
With the soft purr of night as our guide.

Crackle and sigh, let the world fade away,
In the warmth of this night, we choose to stay.
For every ember holds a story's spark,
In the soft purr of whispered dark.

Lanterns Beneath a Copper Dome

Beneath the dome, lanterns sway,
Guiding us through the end of day.
With every flicker, a path is shown,
In shadows cast, we are never alone.

Copper hues dance with flickering light,
Whispers of hope in the approaching night.
As laughter echoes across the square,
Memories linger, weaving through the air.

Each lantern a keeper of stories grand,
Of moments cherished, hand in hand.
Beneath their glow, we take a chance,
In the embrace of joy, we find our dance.

With every step, beneath the stars' gaze,
Together we wander, lost in a haze.
For lanterns guide where our hearts may roam,
Under the copper dome, we are home.

Enchanted Reflections in Glass

Glistening shards of timeless grace,
Reflections dance in a hidden space.
Images swim like dreams in flight,
Echoes of moments, lost in light.

In the glass, we see a spark,
Of laughter shared in the fading dark.
Each surface a story waiting to bloom,
In the quiet magic of a room.

Fragments of past in colors bright,
Capturing echoes in wondrous sight.
As we gaze deeper, realities blend,
In enchanted reflections, old wounds mend.

With every glance, a memory's chance,
To hold on tight, to take a stance.
In the shimmering glass, we see our fate,
Enchanted reflections in life's great state.

Reverie in a Bubble

In a bubble, dreams are spun,
Whispers of laughter, warmth of the sun.
Colors swirl in gentle dance,
Floating softly, lost in a trance.

Moments captured, fragile and bright,
Time stands still in ethereal light.
Voices echo, sweet and clear,
In this realm, nothing to fear.

Bubbles burst, but memories stay,
Like fleeting thoughts at the end of the day.
Hearts entwined in this fragile space,
In the fleeting joy, we find our grace.

A reverie held, an endless flight,
Through the darkness, we chase the light.
In a bubble, life feels right,
Floating softly into the night.

Luminous Brews of Serenity

In a cup, warmth swirls anew,
Luminous brews, kissed by the dew.
Aromatic whispers fill the air,
Serenity found in moments rare.

Steam rises, dancing like dreams,
Life's quiet pleasure, or so it seems.
Sip by sip, the world falls away,
In the solace, we wish to stay.

Colors blend, a palette divine,
Comfort brewed in every line.
Each drop savored, peace ignites,
In luminous moments, we find our sights.

A fragrant journey, heartbeats align,
In the stillness, we dare to unwind.
Serenity cradles, gently we sway,
In luminous brews, we find our way.

Embered Moments Under a Canopy

Under the stars, embers glow bright,
Moments of magic, a soft, warm light.
Beneath the canopy, stories unfold,
Whispers of secrets, both timid and bold.

The crackling fire, a tender embrace,
Illuminating smiles on each upturned face.
Memories made, woven like thread,
In the tapestry of life, where we tread.

Night blooms softly, with shadows that sway,
Crafting a symphony, as night turns to day.
Embered auras, glowing so near,
In these moments, we have nothing to fear.

Together we linger, time slips away,
In the warmth of the fire, we choose to stay.
Under the stars, love's gentle decree,
Embered moments, forever we'll be.

Flickering Glow with Every Pour

In a vessel, warmth does flow,
Flickering glow with every pour.
A dance of flavors, rich and deep,
A moment treasured, ours to keep.

From tepid thoughts to passions bright,
Steam unfurls like a beacon of light.
In each sip, a world to explore,
Flickering glow, inviting us more.

Time unravels, slow and sweet,
As gratitude blooms in every heartbeat.
With every drop, the spirit sings,
Filling our souls with wondrous things.

In shared silence, our lives entwined,
With every pour, new paths we find.
A flickering glow shared in each chore,
In these moments, we ask for no more.

Comfort in a Spout

In the corner, kettle sings,
Steam rises in gentle rings.
Warmth spills forth, a soft embrace,
Comfort found in this small place.

Pouring kindness from its spout,
Filling cups without a doubt.
Each sip whispers quiet dreams,
In the light, where hope redeems.

Friends gather 'round, hearts align,
Stories shared over cups of brine.
In this moment, joy takes flight,
Comfort lingers in the night.

So let the kettle hum its tune,
Underneath the watchful moon.
In the warmth of shared delight,
Find your peace, hold it tight.

Dancing Flames and Stars

In the hearth, the flames do twirl,
Flickering with an airy swirl.
Casting shadows, shapes that play,
Dancing brightly, night and day.

Up above, the stars they gleam,
Winking softly, like a dream.
In the dark, a cosmic dance,
Whispers of a vast expanse.

Fires crackle, stories told,
Of adventures brave and bold.
As constellations spin and weave,
A universe that we believe.

With the flames and stars in sync,
Hearts ignite, we pause and think.
In this rhythm, life unfolds,
A tale of wonder yet untold.

Moonlit Reflection on Ceramics

Under moonlight, porcelain glows,
Smooth and cool, the beauty shows.
Each curve tells a story sweet,
Whispers soft beneath our feet.

Patterns dance in silver light,
Fragile dreams, a pure delight.
Holding memories within their form,
In their presence, hearts stay warm.

Underneath the starry sky,
Elegant pieces catch the eye.
Ceramics cradle, gently hold,
Stories waiting to be told.

So in this moment, still and bright,
Find your peace in soft twilight.
Let reflections guide your way,
In the moon's soft, tender sway.

The Sound of Water's Embrace

Gentle babble of the stream,
Cradling dreams within its gleam.
With each ripple, stories flow,
Whispers of a world below.

Water dances on the stones,
Singing softly, heart at home.
In its embrace, worries cease,
Every drop brings forth a peace.

Echoes blend with nature's song,
In this realm, we all belong.
A melody that calls us near,
Water's voice, forever clear.

So listen close and let it guide,
Feel the waves, let thoughts subside.
In water's arms, life finds its grace,
A sweet embrace, a timeless space.

Flickers of Solace

In twilight's gentle embrace,
Whispers of calm take their place.
Stars begin their nightly dance,
A symphony, a trance.

Moonlight bathes the silent trees,
Carrying soft, soothing pleas.
Each glimmer, a warm caress,
A heart finds its quiet rest.

Moments shared in hushed delight,
Brought together by the night.
In stillness, fear fades away,
Wrapped in peace, we choose to stay.

Glowing Gatherings and Sips

Gather round the flickering fire,
Hearts ignite with shared desire.
Laughter mingles in the air,
Joy unfolds, sweet and rare.

With every sip, warmth flows through,
Stories shared, old and new.
In this circle, we're alive,
Find our strength, together thrive.

The night wraps us in its fold,
Memories made, bright and bold.
With glowing hearts and open eyes,
We embrace the starry skies.

Shadows Cast by Golden Glimmer

As day surrenders to the night,
Shadows stretch in fading light.
Glimmers dance on quiet streams,
Fleeting echoes of our dreams.

Golden hues paint the skies,
Softly whispering goodbyes.
In twilight's grasp, we find our way,
Silent wishes on display.

Each shadow holds a secret tale,
Of joys that rise, of dreams that sail.
In their presence, we're alive,
From darkness, hope will always thrive.

A Harmony of Heat and Light

Sunrise breaks with golden rays,
A gentle start to new days.
Heat wraps us like a warm embrace,
Inviting smiles, a tender grace.

Morning dew on petals gleam,
Nature sings, a lively theme.
In this dance of shadows, bright,
Harmony of heat and light.

As the sun begins to climb,
Moments captured, frozen time.
In every flicker, life ignites,
A world alive with endless sights.

Enchanted Steeps of Time

In valleys deep where shadows play,
Whispers sway in the light of day.
Ancient trees stand firm and tall,
Guardians of secrets, they heed the call.

Stars reveal a story long,
Echoes of laughter, a silent song.
Through winding paths, a journey flows,
In the enchanted steeps, the heart knows.

Moments linger like a soft caress,
Time wraps gently, not in excess.
Each step forward, a breath to claim,
In the dance of seasons, we're all the same.

Let the dawn break with golden hues,
Awake the dreams that time construes.
In the steeps of wonder, find your way,
As echoes of time softly sway.

Emblems of Comfort in Carrying Glow

In twilight's embrace, a candle flickers,
Soft warmth spreads, the heart sticker.
Whispers of love linger in the air,
Emblems of comfort, a tender care.

Together we gather, hands intertwined,
In this glowing circle, our souls aligned.
The world may tremble, but here we stand,
Cradled in warmth, hearts by heart's hand.

Stars above mirror our shared light,
Guiding us through the deepening night.
With every smile, the shadows flee,
In the company of love, we find unity.

Through the ups and downs, in storms, we'll row,
With emblems of comfort, our spirits grow.
Let the ember burn, forever bright,
A beacon of hope in the darkest night.

Trails of Light in Boiling Waters

Among the steam where visions blur,
The paths of light begin to stir.
Every drop tells a tale untold,
In boiling waters, brave hearts behold.

Glistening ripples dance and twine,
Each wave carries the pulse divine.
Through trials faced, foundations shift,
In the heat of struggle, spirits lift.

Beneath the surface, realms collide,
In currents strong, we learn to glide.
Follow the sparks that lead the way,
Through boiling waters, let courage sway.

As twilight descends and echoes fade,
The trails of light we have made.
In every surge, we find our might,
In boiling waters, we chase the light.

Nights Wrapped in Subtle Heat

Under the cover of night's embrace,
Soft whispers linger in tranquil space.
Stars weave dreams in the cool, dark air,
Nights wrapped softly in gentle care.

Moonlight glistens on the silent stream,
Reflecting hopes, cradled in a dream.
Time slows down in this secret retreat,
Where hearts beat softly, and lovers meet.

Beneath the cloak of the velvet sky,
Every sigh holds a world of why.
In the warmth of shadows, two souls entwine,
Embracing the night as their hearts align.

Embers of warmth flicker and glow,
In the depths of night, sweet feelings flow.
Wrapped in comfort, we find our place,
In nights of subtle heat, love leaves its trace.

Sips of Luminescent Joy

In the glass, a shimmer bright,
A dance of flavors, pure delight.
Sip the nectar, sweet and clear,
In each drop, I feel you near.

Golden rays through windows spill,
Wafts of laughter, soft and shrill.
Moments caught in twilight's glow,
Sips of joy, as rivers flow.

Fleeting whispers in the night,
Sparkling dreams, a true insight.
With each dawn, the world awakes,
In this magic, my heart quakes.

Raise your glass, let spirits soar,
For in love, there's always more.
Sips of bliss, forever known,
In luminescence, we are home.

Echoes of Warm Sunshine

Golden rays on weary days,
Whispers heard in playful plays.
Sunbeam's laughter, soft and light,
Echoes boundless, pure delight.

Fields of daisies, gently sway,
In the warmth, lost in the play.
Nature's song, a heart's embrace,
In the sunlight, find your grace.

Memories woven in the breeze,
Drifting softly, with such ease.
Echoes linger, sweet and kind,
In warm sunshine, peace we find.

Moments cherished, never fade,
In the warmth, fears allayed.
With each dawn, let spirits rise,
In soft echoes, love never dies.

The Tinkle of Evening Rituals

In the garden, evening falls,
Gentle tinkles, nature's calls.
A tea set waits beneath the trees,
In twilight's arms, a soft breeze.

Candles flicker, shadows dance,
Moments woven into chance.
In the air, a fragrant mix,
Rituals form, creating fix.

Chimes of laughter linger near,
Echoing memories we hold dear.
As stars peek through the dusky veil,
These evening tales will never pale.

Gather close, let stories flow,
In this warmth, our hearts will glow.
The tinkle sings a soothing tune,
In nightly rituals, love is strewn.

Surreal Nexus of Heat and Light

In the dusk where shadows play,
Heat and light twine, gently sway.
Colors blend in vivid dreams,
A surreal world, or so it seems.

Waves of warmth in every hue,
Moments captured, pure and true.
In the nexus where we meet,
Life unfolds, a rhythmic beat.

Mirrored skies, reflections gleam,
In this magic, hearts redeem.
Breathe the air, electric thrill,
In this nexus, time stands still.

Fleeting visions, soft and bright,
In the dance of heat and light.
Together in this fleeting night,
We find solace, pure delight.